NOTHING
AND
VARIATIONS

poems

NOTHING
AND
VARIATIONS
poems

ANINDITA MUKHERJEE

Hawakal
PUBLISHERS

New Delhi | Calcutta

HAWAKAL PUBLISHERS PRIVATE LIMITED
70 B/9 Amritpuri, East of Kailash, New Delhi 65
33/1/2 K B Sarani, Mall Road, Calcutta 80

Email info@hawakal.com
Website www.hawakal.com

First edition (paperback) July 2022

Cover illustrated by Sudheesh Kottembram

ISBN: 978-93-91431-09-9 (paperback)

Price: INR 150 | USD 10.99

For those
Who are tenebrous

ACKNOWLEDGEMENTS

As the light catches up with innumerable complacencies, and old catastrophes leave the bile in the inkpot, I must count its flow in the cartridge. I am indebted to my teacher and friend Moinak Biswas, who not only opened up a world of poetry with extraordinary subtlety but also made me aware of the austerity and responsibility of writing. I am thankful to friend, teacher and fellow-poet Brinda Bose for her belief in the abundance and impoverishment of my words. I am extremely grateful to my mother who always basked in the empty slate to preserve my flickering essence. Some of the poems in this collection have been written in an enthusiastic creative writing class under the guidance of GJV Prasad in JNU, from whom I have learnt that one writes poetry mostly while rewriting. And I cannot thank Saitya Brata Das enough, my friend-philosopher-guide-confidante, for letting me understand what it takes to give birth to prose, poetry and finally to oneself. I heartily thank Selina, Sampurna, Hyash and my long-standing friends, for their patience and time, otherwise, my words would have lost their first readers. Lastly, without Sudipto, I would never have understood why must poetry push its language to such extremes.

CONTENTS

THEME FOR A JCB

The human species
     can bite on an atom bomb
     with thirty-two teeth.

With luck satisfied
     The wisdom tooths
     can walk like a carrier
     of flabby gums.

It can only bend once
        up and down
     the torso, and tail.

Yama's horns: Hade's bident: austere and unseen
The seasons of JCB
           biting bodies below
     almost thirty feet deep.
It can bend thrice
        in interstellar space: *Dhapar Math*

Cerberus is full and polite
The buffalo crowds my blindness.

KALEIDOSCOPE

Through a mirror's passage
        I built the symmetry of wind
                with gulf and prophecy

I keep awake —
        with blind monotony
                creasing my diaphanous breath.

                The unjust hands
                work for words
                Sign they look for —
                is the grig's collapse —

CALCUTTA, MON AMOUR

When you hint at monastic ruins
                It's more you than the dead sea
It is less time carrying away more
than it brings close
More than closure.

Feeling time is
                not time passing
Neither can passing time be passed.

I am distilling time in a sand-glass —

which is older than Alexandria and Miletus.
more in my head than all of life in poetry.

She is free of the squabble of voices
        but caught in the mood of her own: Calcutta coxcombs.

nothing immediate or blunted
neither imitative
                        but can be self-taught like a poet.

It must be so —

As members of maturity
  teasing an unmistakable idiom
like a new war in greased clang —

Stripped to the feeling bone
I don't have the cadence
for a touch unabashed.

The gunfire mornings
     closes with words
You are tired with sleep savage.

Languor, refusal —
It was elsewhere, untranslatable —

BEHIND THE NAME, SPHINX

The head the body learns to pose
toys in wings and tails
as aesthetic archetype
as if a joke of bullet holes
a hollow puzzle
you see
but cannot peer.
Look if some
form of Omega
and Alpha
rhyme as common names
lopping the extremes
called *Chimera*
or *Or-thus*
without flight of claws
in a perch.
The nucleus of
absolute act
is not the riddle.
Once played
conformed in a drapery
as transparent
as black.

The riddle
gonged in labyrinths and reflections
is but a monochrome
licked on ashes to taste fire.
Avenues as delirious
as incandescent reticence
audible shrieks from tombstones
You just think you hear Dirges and Death Songs
have similitudes.
The cryptonym
of my death
is a riddle.
Human insufficiencies are
not printed in blood.
Through lungs and nostrils —
The ashes in the wind
are my riddles —

IF I TOLD YOU, I COMPLETED PACKING DUST

I
Fiction is like the woollen scarf.
Poems have seen dust in the sea's night.
I have put them back in the suitcase.

II
The mump and maculate V-fixed collar, thrusted by
the first cousin of winter- pullover.
Nothing quixotic, a spectacle strange inside a
disengaged hurt.
Unordered, resembling the unspreading. I have put
them back in the suitcase.

III
They are at peace. Some of them have sold their
warmth, as a sovereign humble contagion.
Cascading like rough brushes. I have put them back
in the suitcase.

IV
A long dying ends with a plundered glove. I forgot
to caress its lustre.

The embrace of oranges and scarce love. As you look
here, distressed silence.
I have put them back in the suitcase.

V

They didn't fit well. Said they don't belong. Together.
You are thinking of your valentine.
I have put them back in the suitcase.

VI

My socks felt differently about the robust earbuds. It
wasn't windy inside. You just think it
isn't. I have put them back in the suitcase.

VII

Dispelled woollen bundles after cold trysts
Ruins and faceless necks
I had put them back in the suitcase.

LETTER MUSE

Incoherence is not   One Word.
 It's in Coherence.
You climb upon the edifice of one letter
 beginning with a hill
 broken with a dash

                        That is: **A**.

Not A in estuary
 but A in Alone
The first line sings like A
The second remembers.
Be kind: To Letters
An almost made-up Poem
got sadder: it began to know
why You cannot begin with the dash
Slant it off a while
and leave it as Happy Death: **Z**
I am visited by life and rhyme
huddling like two goldfish in plain water.
I wait patiently for them to yawn
They stare at me when it's truly time.
There is no other way to think about them
Scream:
                Be Silent.
They will become   quiet
in
another
way.

MY NAME, ARIADNE

Allow your desires, if you may,
to unravel right beside me, struggle to open
the sarcophagi and clean with privileged arms
the dust, the slate and lance.

I mercy you years
and age seconded with love gone dry. Take a word —
One for summer
and another for an era
piled with thousands of pallid masks.

I reckon a truth
one old, and another new
one history, the other mythology.
one of attack, another of abandonment.

I, the daughter of King Menos of Crete a beacon for
Theseus once
full of mirrors and seasons of gaze so a labyrinth could
he penetrate.
with victory and me he sailed away
only to return me back with a handful of solitude.
The beacon, once having guided home, lay flickering in

the island of Naxos,
along miraculous seas.

I no longer know the pain I shun
One being love, the other appeasement,
The caverns in a fable still
to make me immortal one
Who a moment before a mortal was.

Bended
      Bare
            Metamorphosed
                  An unholy chalice for
            every man
    who made holy my urn
    My name, Ariadne.
    Immortal made A mother
    then goddess
    And next a vegetative state.

Greeks made a mortal again.
a babe seized and passed
One a Dionysian impulse,
and another a Theseusian pulsation.

The sleeping half, with Dionysus at bay Thiasos too
joined,
late —
Poured cups and libation
while I lay
 peered curves and relics glared
with ambrosia nay.

We are never loved while in love

more when bewitched surmises imprisoned high.

Spilled and rested in dark shivering twilight
Cupped in Campanion wall painting
Stilted, washed, brushed
laid in conical fingers, managed with ink well,
kissed in confused lament,
Once, Only,
in a truly diminishing love.

My best body is in sleep built
in art,
empty.

TASTE OF BUDS

From the bullet dots of my
CV
If tastebuds
translate
A feast for speech
Remember
the lemon-skin
squeezed
in
one of those eyes.
It's not just bitter
but a moment of peering a whole burn
Letting it
wipe away
As stories unfold
of beauty and love
bearing Eros
on my tongue.
In the end
I pause
Tongues telling higher mysteries
are dangerously created
at the end of

letters —
alphabets —
Signs: *kalous logous*

We recall
the previous toils
sudden-wondrous
as if there is
no other knowing
than the
knowledge of me
words that fed
and was fed upon: *elenchus*

The one language I knew
is unknown to the bed-stead.
To put it differently —
The tongue
in a wild space
a Muse
in a museum
The uvula
in strife
Love & Wisdom.
I remain
the underbelly
without a
disciple: Diotima.

THE NAME OF THOU

Hazy indolences on the parapet
indistinct swarms of finger nails
eagerly passed between
moles and nimble knees

The house of age and black sleep
wandering for dying touch
is the dove's unbecoming

The earth's skeleton
perishes in distant time.

The secret of the craft
abyss
and exile embroidered
in disarming pain

It drips
in gracious desire
like an ancient colosseum

Slowness: drunken *dingi*
Caress: Ophelia bare

Prisms / Petrichor

Double on the leeching aeon

       rankle the empty quest

sit beside the window hearth

       Mirror on the length of a thought

stay uncertain, banished

Know the continual whirl

       amidst the yellow unearth.

THEMSELVES

In the remainder of life, thinned out
        a soft colour departs
                like the whistling train

                laboured love: stretched out
        with no true trace.
The face of you
the filaments
receding lids
in the interstice of grim brows.

ahr you my conhieus?

Silicon spume
of dry dust
drapery of a cut-out cloak

Chiaroscuro
turquoise blood
ultramarine sighs
                        of autumn afternoons

Unto you, are verses, vacuums!

THE ART OF GREY

Unconsumate the vogue
        covers and sprinklers
Sobriety of the clay saucer

Undo the written woe
        the muddy sidewalks of Milena and
Bachmann

Unsavour the kitsch, squall
                winged imago

Unbridle, pour the impossible
        and exhaust endless

        Put one eye against the mouth: ocular orgasm

BEFORE I COULD CALL MYSELF POSTHUMOUS

The poets of daybreak
thrive in excesses —
faults rift in
aborted seals.

Cities merge
over cable wires
languorous armchairs
in swift mezzanine floors
receive the sun —
obedient gestures of
escapades
play the part
of the act
you hold
in premises
between the thumb and index finger —
withdraws to the brief button
of your shirt.

You tie
to untie

without summoning
the embers
that *Icchamoti* drowns.

I corner
the thick weeping of maladies.

Two cities
now speak of death
in discrete chambers
ashes and fowls
fly
under the chorus of
Azaan
pitched in
beguiling twigs
of mornings
yielding hieroglyphics
of an old
mournful love.

The nameless burning
under the lamp of
biting beds
stuck between the sky and
the sky alone.

Your posthumous essence
churns
lines imperceptible
and mists that
quiver outside
window panes.

Memory and desire
once mixed
subsists
scarcely with sullen weight.

You become a place of no place
a place yet not place
a farce yet not verse
about winters that fail to
arrive on time.

I am your
sagging Olympus
voluptuously flesh
that carry afternoon storms —
the burdens of a poet —
and indecisions of a whore
that must once
belie
breasts, bellies and sunflowers.

Tomorrow begins in
abacuses
eclipses —
I have forgotten
epithets, vowels, consonants
that lynch rhetoric
out in frivolous neglect.

Tomorrow, the delirious
ferment of passions
carry inklings of your gaze
in vanishing rafters.

Am I the carriage?

Echo of April
and June
that gnaws
and whispers
of doubly counted dispersal —
breeds lilacs and burns hyacinths
of one name
I slept with.

Arching with another night
frosted on a bitumen lament.

I believe cities
scatter in quietness
winds bite wounds
pollens and black blues
leaf after leaf.

I won't disappear
in twenty yards of echo
warm tongue-hours
mounds of rest, form, times
Either/or
into the laborious infinite of
the saddle.

That I am
word and voice
no motor you have
now that
posthumous you claim.

My feverish hands

recognize
the nocturnal pity and
retreating heels

Flows Magdalene's tears
with minutes of the last act.
I see strange waistcoats
black umbrellas
to sway the autopsy
of our posthumous liaison.
I swell with blind purpose
and drink
melting ravines.

EPISTLES: FOR PASOLINI

The loveless —

>   I tremble in peace, search again-
>   never-never betwixt the sea and sailor
>   has an anguished gale
>   returned its rhythm
>   rage against the old phantom
>   come whip on the waves
>
>   Willy-nilly
>   faraway Friuli —
>
>   skip the stupendous monotony of mariners
>   those who atones sins
>   with round-headed bullets
>   scurrying cemetery rats
>
>   I abandoned myself to the blindman's songs
>   with the equal source
>   of sleep
>   a slender flexible visage

The faithful —

Brief: for Pasolini

To return —

        The real remorse
        is not the end of a Roman holiday.
        The candle road attends longer.

        Romanesque love
        returns to
        Terzina
        for supper in hollow concealments
        in a tomb
        under
        wet resounding wheels
        that lament for a city
        of love past.

        A necessary return
        is a blot on the livery
        I cannot return unwashed of history

                The deferred —

OZI: FOR PASOLINI

The black rage —
    Small deaths and deadly laughs
    spurred at
    Transtevere station
    pukes of
    evenings sweet.
    The treasures
    that guided road
    in confusion rake —
    tough
    sturdy
    for kids
    with guns
    blow ashes
    black as the darkened lips
    I rage against the
    Cymbal's core
    White is the
    confusion of the soul
                The twitches —

CHITHI: FOR PASOLINI

The steps
            White sheets
defend the
picked up deserts.
Facades and cobwebs
of comets,
pillow-covers
that
overgrow the dungeons
both sincere and debauch

The stupendous self
inconsistent with expression
of a known life
claims anonymity
till I discovered misnomers
of the world
dying to the silences
of a miserable truth
            The eluded —

LETERO: FOR PASOLINI

The fear —
               I ain't asleep
               echoes in wheels
               returning home
               burn peaceful stables.
               Disfigured walls
               Wine bars
               set ablaze
               make me run
               through choked air
               and rubbles of a city
               I called soul
               and lived.

               Whatever loved
               was not fear
               but longer to know
               whatever now
               is fear

               It echoes
               and sings too.
                              Identical tears —

LÈT: FOR PASOLINI

The hunger —
> The fate of light
> is the red of
> empty stomachs,
> crafted well
> in post-war epics
> which rages and cries
> relapses in
> future
> Hence
> Hunger
> is lost
> among
> ruins.

> > The morsel —

LETËR: FOR PASOLINI

The absent hymn —
       These letters
       in stilted stones
       obedient
       to be written:
       Écriture
       Feed no more
       to the anxious
       who is not free

         the solemnity —

PRESENTIMENT

'There is a secret argument between the past generation and the present one'

— Walter Benjamin

A single bed. On top a turquoise charm.
Spread on four legs of afterlives
under a crackling ceiling fan
mornings break in shanty rags

Beyond the lunch hour
the evening dreads.

Rear grooves of pink,
or, I colour of warm scents
I don't remember.
Mystic dreamers wrapped in
yellow wallpaper,
whirling on the blades
made slow by summer
Iridescent —
steaked with
the ambush

Warding off silence
cloaks the trivial and profound.

A sink creaks
as one strikes the gray-blue mists.

The lone-some
the lazy shades
lapped into
the wall-holes

A secret plan
like every wall-hanging
dissolving figures of a museum
where
l'avenir bounds in turns

The wire
cracks on wet walls
hold the plaintive cry

Tomorrow seems to lower
the labouring present.

The sand
and I
kitchen and Sink
rust and steel.

EXQUISITE HOUR
*"Our image of happiness is indissolubly bound up with the image
of the past"*
— Walter Benjamin

I found
the firmament
under the bowers

I picked up
the joyous
erratic and unfamiliar cornea

A vision
of mornings
twilight
and blue moon.

THE VERDICT
"Nothing that has ever happened should be regarded as lost for history"
— Walter Benjamin

A lunar dice
despondent
living paper knives
with paper trinkets

Be it the
bulletin or
slopes of jargon
the fly reads it.

Stuck with a small weight
the paper unreaps.

There is only
one true thing
Blunt fables
and your sense

Two indeed —

IN THE UNENDING
"But a storm is blowing from Paradise"
— Walter Benjamin

I stand upon the tiles
in false armour

Only skin
and nails
and Eve.

In the depths of Adam's heart
I am his ribs.

I stand afar
I grow with the dead.

THE TEDIUM
"For every second of time was the strait gate through which the Messiah might enter"
> — Walter Benjamin

Woe is without strife

weighed down by the
Hour of his coming.

The worm eats
what is forbidden

I am the weak power

Waiting in dark
flagellated birds
faced with future
Depart.

THE AFTERTHOUGHT

This is an afterthought of union, not abandonment,
this is an afterthought of arrival, not departure.
Do I lie turtle-turned? Then let me.
Do logs and longings bend? Let them bend.

Tomorrow or day after the pebble's split will exactly be here
Supinely will I swim, baring the bosom;
Come funeral-friends, this is the knotted repair,
the wood-hay, the wanton readiness
The aeonian anguish, the enduring hecatomb of love.